The Hunchback of Notre-Dame

VICTOR HUGO
Translated by Walter J. Cobb

Level 3

Retold by Nancy Taylor
Series Editors: Andy Hopkins and Jocelyn Potter

Pearson Education Limited
Edinburgh Gate, Harlow,
Essex CM20 2JE, England
and Associated Companies throughout the world

ISBN: 978-1-4058-5550-1

First published by Penguin Books 2004
This edition published 2008

3 5 7 9 10 8 6 4

Original translation copyright © 1965 by Walter J. Cobb
Text copyright © Penguin Books Ltd 2004
This edition copyright © Pearson Education Ltd 2008
Illustrations by Nick Harris (Virgil Pomfret)

Typeset by Graphicraft Ltd, Hong Kong
Set in 11/14pt Bembo
Printed in China
SWTC/03

Produced for the Publishers by Bluestone Press, Charlbury, Oxfordshire, UK

Published by Pearson Education Ltd in association with
Penguin Books Ltd., both companies being subsidiaries of Pearson Plc

For a complete list of the titles available in the Penguin Readers series please write to your local
Pearson Longman office or to: Penguin Readers Marketing Department, Pearson Education,
Edinburgh Gate, Harlow, Essex CM20 2JE, England.

Contents

Introduction

Father Claude named the poor child Quasimodo and gave him a home in the cathedral. The boy could not exist in the outside world, but with the priest's help he made a life inside the walls of Notre-Dame.

The idea for one of his greatest books, *Notre-Dame de Paris*, came to Victor Hugo when he was still in his twenties, on a visit to the Cathedral of Notre-Dame. This wonderful church excited the young writer and he placed it at the center of the action. It plays an important part in the lives of the three main people in the book: Quasimodo, the hunchback; Esmeralda, the beautiful gypsy girl; and Father Claude Frollo, the lost priest. It is a sanctuary and a prison for all of them.

As a young priest, Claude Frollo finds his life's work in the cathedral. It is a sanctuary where he can study and work. He becomes a proud, successful churchman. But suddenly, after many years, he feels a need to escape from his life as a priest. Notre-Dame has become a prison that stops him finding love.

The cathedral is a prison for Quasimodo, too, because he cannot live outside it. He is ugly and different, and people are afraid of him. He is safe and happy inside its walls with Father Claude and with the great bells of Notre-Dame. But he also wants more from life.

The hunchback and the priest exist together in the cathedral until Esmeralda arrives. Without knowing it, the gypsy girl brings pain and suffering into their quiet lives. Notre-Dame also plays a large part in her story. It offers her sanctuary, but is also a prison. Death waits for her outside.

In English, this book is known as *The Hunchback of Notre-Dame*. For most modern readers, this is a good title. Quasimodo is the person in the story that we remember most clearly. He has problems and pain that we can understand. We want him to find happiness, but is this possible in his dark, lonely world?

Victor Hugo was born in 1802 in Besançon, France. He lived through an exciting time in the history and literature of his country.

Victor's father was a soldier who became a general under Napoleon. The young boy traveled with him until he was ten. After that his mother kept her three sons in Paris and put them in good schools. Victor was an excellent student and at seventeen he won an important prize for his poems. He received money from the government of King Louis XVIII after he wrote his first complete book of poems in 1822.

In that year, he also married Adèle Foucher. Their home became a meeting place for young French writers from the Romantic school of writing. This group wanted to change French literature by moving away from the style of the past. They wanted their stories, their plays, and their poems to show the importance of strong feelings. People's lives were more important to these writers than big ideas. Their imagination guided them, but they also used history. By describing important times in the history of their countries, these writers made their work more serious and more interesting to a large number of people.

Victor Hugo's two most popular books in English follow the ideas of this group of Romantic writers. *The Hunchback of Notre-Dame* (1831) is about three people's lives, but it also tells the reader a lot about life in Paris in 1482. *Les Misérables* (1862), also a Penguin Reader, follows the life of one man, Jean Valjean. This time, the reader learns a lot about France in the early years of the 1800s.

In France, Victor Hugo is remembered for his many books and plays, and also as a politician. But more than anything, Hugo is remembered in his own country as one of the greatest writers of poems of all time. When he died in 1885, the French government remembered his life at a state service. After this special service, three million people followed his body to its final resting place.

Why does *The Hunchback of Notre-Dame* continue to be popular in the English-speaking world? First, the story and the people are important to us. Quasimodo is different from other people and he has suffered. But we believe there is room in the world for someone like him. His feelings are strong and true, and we want happiness for him. We also understand Esmeralda's life. Until the last minute, we hope that she will escape from her terrible problems.

Second, the story is exciting. There is good and evil, love and hate, life and death. Some people are kind and others are bad, but they are all real. We understand their actions. We want to find out how their stories will end.

Sometimes writers have changed Victor Hugo's ending to the story. There have been five different movies of *The Hunchback of Notre-Dame*. The first one came out in 1923. The Disney company made a movie in 1996. Try to see it after you read this book. It is interesting to compare the two endings. Which one do you think is better?

Chapter 1   A Day of Surprises

On the morning of January 6, 1482, the streets of Paris are crowded. It is the last day of the Christmas season and the people of the capital are ready for a party. There will be singing and dancing, and later a big fire with plenty of food in the Place de Grève. But now the people are hurrying to the Great Hall for the first and most amusing activity of the day. Everyone wants to find a good place to watch a new play. They also want to be able to see the important politicians, college professors, and churchmen in the seats above them.

At noon, the people begin shouting, "The play! The play! We want the play!" And after a few minutes the play begins. The writer of the play, Pierre Gringoire, is listening very carefully. Today the most important people in Paris are hearing his words. The young man dreams that he will be famous, and possibly even rich, by the end of the afternoon.

Suddenly, the actors stop speaking. Every face in the crowd turns to watch the greatest churchman of Paris, a close friend of King Louis XI, arrive in the theater with a group of ten or twelve other important men. When these people are finally sitting down, the play continues. But after a few minutes one of the churchman's guests, a rich Belgian businessman from Ghent, shouts, "Excuse me, good people of Paris, what are we doing here? Today's a day for parties and fun, but I'm not amused. What's this play about? The problems of old politicians and priests. It's boring, don't you agree?

"My friends," the businessman continues, "it's time to choose your 'Pope★ of Fools.' In my country on the sixth of January, we

★ Pope: the head of the Roman Catholic Church

1

play a game to choose our Pope. It's a lot more fun than this boring play."

Everyone shouts happily and one student calls out, "Tell us how to play the game, good sir!"

"It's really very easy. If you want to be Pope, you come up to the stage. One by one you put your heads through a hole in a sheet. We choose the person who can make the ugliest face."

The crowd loves the game. They laugh as one strange face after another pushes through the hole. But suddenly the crowd is silent. They have seen some very ugly faces, but now they are clearly looking at the winner. The face has a nose like a big potato, a wide mouth in the shape of a horseshoe, a small left eye under heavy red hair, a closed right eye, and a few very large and broken teeth. It also has a look that seems dangerous and sad at the same time.

"The Pope! The Pope!" shouts the crowd. A few students pull down the sheet and the people see their Pope.

"Oh, it's Quasimodo. What an ugly thing he is!" one person says. "He's strong, too. He can kill you with two fingers."

"Don't look!" shouts another. "He's as ugly as a wild animal."

Quasimodo is famous in this part of Paris because he rings the bells at the Cathedral of Notre-Dame. His body, like his big face and head, is terrible to look at. He has very large hands and feet, and strangely shaped legs that come together at the knees. The big hump on his back has given him the name the "Hunchback of Notre-Dame." He cannot hear so nobody talks to him. In fact, nobody goes near him. The good people of Paris are afraid of Quasimodo. They believe the stories they have heard about him: He is evil.

But the businessman from Ghent is very pleased. "This is surely the ugliest man in Paris. You've chosen a good Pope."

The students run to the stage with a gold paper hat and coat for their Pope of Fools. They put him on a chair and lift him on their shoulders. Then they carry him through the streets of the city, with

They have seen some very ugly faces, but now they are clearly looking at the winner.

the crowd from the Great Hall following behind. Nobody asks Quasimodo for his opinion of all this, but his ugly face looks almost happy.

At the Great Hall, Pierre Gringoire sits sadly in the empty theater. He knows that his dream is at an end. "Nobody listened to my play. Nobody paid me any money. They chose to listen to a foreigner from Ghent, and now they've followed a hunchback through the streets. What shall I do now?"

Night comes early in Paris at the beginning of a new year. The sky is already dark when the young writer reaches the Place de Grève. He is hoping to get warm at the big fire and to find some free food. He is also worried about a bed for the night because he cannot return to his apartment. He hasn't paid the owner of the building for the last six months, and the man is waiting for his money.

The writer walks toward the big fire in the middle of the square, but he cannot get near it. A crowd of people is watching a beautiful young gypsy girl. She sings and dances like someone from a different world. Gringoire pushes to the front of the crowd for a closer look. The girl has dark gold skin and very black hair, and eyes that shine brightly in her beautiful face. In her colorful gypsy dress, she moves like a foreign princess from an old storybook.

Every face in the crowd watches the girl, but a quiet, serious man seems to study her very closely. This man is wearing a long black coat and his pale face has deep lines, maybe from worry or from study. He is already losing his hair, but he is probably only about thirty-five years old. His eyes never leave the girl's face, but he does not seem to enjoy watching her.

Finally, the girl stops dancing and the crowd begins to shout, "Don't stop, Esmeralda! We want more!"

Esmeralda, the gypsy girl, calls for Djali, her pretty white goat.

"Djali," says the dancer, "now it's your turn. What day of the month is it?"

The goat lifts one little foot and hits the ground six times.

"And what time is it?" asks Esmeralda.

Djali hits the ground seven times, and then the clock on the church rings seven o'clock.

"This is evil," shouts a voice in the crowd. It is the man in the long black coat. But the crowd wants more.

"Djali," says the girl, "how does Monsieur* Charmolue, the King's lawyer, walk?"

The goat walks on two legs, exactly like Monsieur Charmolue. Everyone laughs and shouts for more.

But the same serious man cries again, "The girl is evil, and that goat is a devil."

Esmeralda turns her head. "Oh, it's that terrible man. Why does he follow me everywhere? Why does he hate me?"

Then the crowd hears another voice. "Go away, gypsy girl. We don't want you here." This time it is not the man in the black coat. It is a woman's voice, full of hate.

"It's Sachette, the witch from the Tower of Roland," shout some children.

The witch has locked herself in the Tower of Roland at one corner of the Place de Grève. She hates all gypsy women. She shouts at them when they come near her prison.

The people forget about Sachette when they hear loud noises at the entrance to the square. The Pope of Fools and a great crowd of thieves and gypsies run into the Place de Grève.

Quasimodo has no friends, and he has never known love, but today he is a king. It is exciting to be part of the people's great day of fun and parties. His heart is filled with happiness for the first time in his short, painful life.

It is no surprise that Quasimodo's happiness does not last long. The same quiet man in the black coat hurries out of the crowd.

* Monsieur, Madame, Mademoiselle: the French words for Mr., Mrs., and Miss

5

With an angry face, he pulls the gold hat and coat from the hunchback and throws them to the ground.

Gringoire knows this man. "It's Father Claude Frollo, an important priest from Notre-Dame!" he says to himself. "Is he crazy? Quasimodo will break him into little pieces."

Everyone waits for the hunchback to throw Father Claude to the ground. They know he is very strong. But Quasimodo falls on his knees in front of the priest and the two men speak by using hand signs. Then they leave the square silently and disappear down a dark, narrow street. Nobody follows them because everyone is afraid of Quasimodo.

"This has been a day of surprises: a beautiful gypsy girl, an ugly hunchback, a terrible priest, and a crazy witch," thinks Pierre Gringoire. "But where am I going to find supper and a bed?" He is now very hungry and cold, so he decides to follow the beautiful gypsy girl.

"She probably has a warm little house for herself and her goat," thinks the writer. "And I've heard that gypsies are good, kind people. Who knows...?"

Esmeralda and Djali walk quickly down a number of dark, lonely streets. Gringoire does not know this part of Paris. Soon he is lost, but he continues to follow the pretty pair. Then Esmeralda turns a corner and for a minute Gringoire cannot see her. He hears a loud female scream and runs to the corner.

The street is dark except for one small light in a narrow window. In the shadows, Gringoire can see the gypsy fighting with two men who are trying to carry her away.

"Help! Help! Police!" shouts Gringoire. He hurries toward Esmeralda, but one of the men turns and sees him. It is Quasimodo. The hunchback hits Gringoire. The young writer flies across the road and hits his head on the hard sidewalk. His eyes close and everything goes black.

"Murder! Murder!" screams the poor gypsy.

A group of soldiers suddenly arrives in the road.

"Stop, you criminals! Don't touch that woman!" shouts an officer of the King's Guard.

The handsome young soldier lifts Esmeralda out of Quasimodo's arms and places her in front of him on his horse. The surprised hunchback tries to attack the officer, but is stopped by fifteen of the officer's men. They catch Quasimodo, tie his hands behind his back, and take him away. The soldiers do not notice a second man, in a black coat, disappearing at the end of the street.

Esmeralda sits nicely on the officer's horse. She turns, places her two hands on the young man's shoulders, and looks at him closely for a few seconds. Then in her sweetest voice she says, "Kind officer, what is your name?"

"Phoebus de Châteaupers, at your service, my pretty lady," answers the officer of the King's Guard.

Esmeralda smiles and looks into the handsome man's eyes. "Thank you," she says softly.

Officer Phoebus smiles and smoothes his mustache. The girl silently climbs off the horse and disappears into the night.

"That was a beautiful girl!" says Phoebus de Châteaupers. "I wanted to keep her."

The dark street is silent and empty now except for one body which is lying next to the sidewalk. Gringoire's clothes are wet and cold, and slowly he begins to wake up. "What happened?" he asks himself. Then he remembers Esmeralda and thinks, "I hope she escaped from that terrible hunchback."

The young writer gets up and begins walking again, but he is completely lost. When the streets end, he finds himself on a wet, dirty road. He is not alone. Here and there he can see strange black shapes moving down the road. Then he sees a red light in the sky. "Oh, wonderful!" cries Gringoire. "A fire and maybe some food."

Now, with the light from the fire, Gringoire can see the black shapes more clearly. One is a man who cannot see. Another is a

"Kind officer, what is your name?"

woman with a bad arm. Then there is a man who cannot walk. All the poor, the weak, and the sick of Paris are moving slowly and painfully down this road. They pull at Gringoire's coat and ask for money, but he does not stop.

Finally, he reaches the end of the road and finds himself in a great square with a thousand lights and a crowd of noisy people. Everyone is suddenly strong and healthy when they arrive at the square.

"Where am I?" asks Gringoire.

"You're in the City of Thieves," answers a man in the clothes of a soldier. He is cleaning red paint from his head. Tomorrow, he will put more "blood" on his head. Then he will return to the city streets to ask for money from the good people of Paris.

"What are *you* doing here?" asks an old thief. "You're not one of us."

"I'm very sorry," begins Gringoire nervously. He knows that even the police are afraid to walk into the City of Thieves. "I'm lost. I was looking for a place to sleep and something to eat."

"You looked in the wrong place this time," the old man laughs.

"Let's take him to the king!" one of the women shouts, and everyone agrees.

The crowd pushes and pulls Gringoire to a large hall at one side of the square. Inside, people are drinking beer and eating at long tables. The King of Thieves is sitting at the best table.

"Who's our pretty friend?" asks the king. "Has he come for a cup of tea and a cookie?"

Everyone laughs at the king's joke, but Gringoire is shaking from head to toe.

"Dear sir, great King..." he tries to say.

"Stop!" shouts the king. He is serious now. "Tell us your name and nothing more."

"I'm Pierre Gringoire. I'm a writer."

"Enough! You've found the City of Thieves, and you're not one of us. I'm your judge. You're not a thief, so we'll punish you. We'll hang you. We'll enjoy that."

"But, good sir…" Gringoire tries again, "I wrote a play. Maybe you saw it today in the Great Hall."

"Yes, I did. It was boring, but your death will be amusing. Is everything ready for a hanging?" the king asks his men.

But then the king thinks of something. "I forgot one of our laws," he says. "Is there a woman here who wants this man for her husband? A man for nothing. If you marry him, he won't die."

"No! No! Hang him! We'll enjoy it," shouts the crowd.

But then a pretty voice is heard at the back of the room. "Are you really going to hang that man?"

"Yes, sister," answers the King of Thieves. "Or will you take him for your husband?"

Esmeralda stops and thinks. "I'll take him," she says.

Gringoire cannot believe his luck. Is this beautiful gypsy really going to save him?

Esmeralda takes his hand, and the king says, "Brother, she is your wife. Sister, he is your husband for four years. Now, go!"

In a few minutes, Gringoire is sitting at a table opposite the beautiful gypsy in a warm little room. There is food in front of him and a good bed in the next room.

The writer looks at the girl and thinks, "She saved my life and married me. She clearly loves me a lot, doesn't she?" With this idea in his head, he touches Esmeralda's hand.

"What do you want with my hand?" she asks, and moves away from Gringoire.

"But you love me. You're my wife," explains the writer.

"Don't be silly. You have no reason to touch me," says Esmeralda.

"But why did you marry me?"

"I didn't want you to die. We can be friends. That's all. Like brother and sister and nothing more. Remember that."

"That's fine for me," says Gringoire. "I'm happy to be alive and warm, and this bread and cheese is delicious. Don't you want something to eat?"

"No, I'm thinking about love," answers Esmeralda.

"What's love?" asks the writer. He always enjoys this kind of conversation.

"Love!" the girl says. "That's when two become one. A man and a woman are joined."

"What kind of man will you love, Esmeralda?" asks Gringoire.

"A soldier on a horse. A man who can protect me. You know about words. What does *Phoebus* mean?" she asks.

"It's a Latin word which means 'sun'," explains Gringoire.

"The sun! How wonderful!" says Esmeralda. Then she forgets about Gringoire and begins to dream. In a minute or two, she disappears into her bedroom and locks the door behind her.

"This isn't a very romantic wedding night," Gringoire says to himself, "but it's much better than dying in the City of Thieves."

Chapter 2   Broken Hearts and Broken Lives

Father Claude Frollo was not an ordinary child. He was born in 1446, and from an early age he was interested in books and learning. He started college very young, learned quickly, and graduated at the age of eighteen. His greatest interests in life were science and religion.

The important men in the Church noticed this serious young man. When he was only twenty years old, they made him a priest. People heard stories of Claude's great learning and, as usual in those days, it worried them. They began to ask themselves if Father Claude was a good priest or an evil sorcerer.

This question was asked openly on Quasimodo Sunday (the first Sunday after Easter), 1467. On that fine morning, a box was left at the main doors of the Cathedral of Notre-Dame. As they were leaving the early church service, two old women looked inside the box.

"What's *that*?" asked the first old lady. "Is it a strange animal? It can't be a child. It's too ugly!"

"Throw it in the river," suggested the second old lady.

By this time, a crowd was looking at the poor little boy. He was crying and was probably hungry and afraid. But nobody wanted to touch the ugly little red-haired, one-eyed hunchback, and clearly nobody wanted to take him home.

Then the young priest, Father Claude Frollo, pushed silently through the crowd. His face was serious and his eyes looked very bright. He put his hand on the forest of red hair and the child stopped crying.

"I'll have this child," said the priest. He picked the boy up and carried him into the cathedral.

After the door closed, one of the old ladies said, "I told you that young priest was a sorcerer. Now do you believe me?"

Father Claude named the poor child Quasimodo and gave him a home in the cathedral. The boy could not exist in the outside world, but with the priest's help he made a life inside the walls of Notre-Dame. Father Claude was very patient and taught the boy to speak, to read, and to write. Quasimodo became part of that great church. He climbed into every corner and knew every piece of wood, glass, and stone.

Ten years after their first Sunday together, when Quasimodo was fourteen, Father Claude found a job for the boy. He became one of the bellringers up in the highest part of the cathedral. Quasimodo loved his job and soon became the chief bellringer, but as usual life was not kind to the hunchback. The sound of the great bells destroyed his hearing. Another door closed for him, and he fell deeper into his own dark world. He stopped speaking and only talked to Father Claude in hand signs.

"I'll have this child," said the priest.

Few people ever saw Quasimodo. When they did, they felt afraid. They believed that he was a devil. They also believed that his helper was Father Claude, the sorcerer. The poor hunchback knew what people thought of him. He hid away and tried to be happy in his world, the Cathedral of Notre-Dame.

Quasimodo was happiest in the bell tower. The bells were his family. He touched them, talked to them, and understood them. Their voices were the only ones that he could still hear. His favorite was Marie, the biggest and best bell, but on special days the bellringers rang all of the fifteen bells. Quasimodo guided his assistants and watched and listened. The sound of the bells lit up his eyes and woke the love in his heart. He ran around and got more and more excited. Finally, he jumped on Marie. He rode her as she sang her wonderful song. As he flew through the air on her back, the hunchback became half man and half bell.

Quasimodo had his cathedral, his bells, and one other love: the priest, Father Claude Frollo. Father Claude took him in, fed him, taught him, and gave him a purpose. The good people of Paris hated Quasimodo, but Father Claude protected him from them. The priest was sometimes silent and his rules were often hard. But Quasimodo loved this man. He would happily give his life to help Father Claude.

And what about the priest? Little by little, between 1467 and 1482, Father Claude became even more serious and even more alone. He continued to study, and he followed the Church's rules for priests very carefully. But people were afraid of him and told dangerous stories about him: "He visits the dead." "He works for the devil." "He is an evil sorcerer."

The priest did have secrets, but nobody understood them. Why was his hair already gray? Why did he always cover his head when he was outside? Why did he keep his eyes on the ground? When did he begin to hate and fear women? And why did he keep gypsy women away from Notre-Dame?

Let us return to 1482 and a courtroom in Paris. It is January 7, and Quasimodo stands in front of Judge Florian Barbedienne. What is his crime? He tried to carry off the gypsy girl, Esmeralda, and he attacked the King's Guard.

Florian Barbedienne is an unusual judge. He cannot hear, not even the bells of Notre-Dame. He is a successful judge because he can read a criminal's face. He sends the bad to prison, and the good are sent home. The judge moves from question to question. Each time he thinks that Quasimodo has answered. But the hunchback has not heard the questions, and soon the people in the courtroom begin to laugh.

Judge Barbedienne sees them laughing. Quasimodo, he thinks, has answered impolitely. But Quasimodo has not said anything.

"Silence!" shouts the judge. Then he turns to the court secretary and asks, "Have you written down the criminal's answers?"

The judge sees the people laugh again and he grows angrier. Quasimodo is the only silent person in the courtroom.

"Hunchback," Judge Barbedienne begins, "I'm very unhappy with your answers. You haven't been serious in my courtroom. I'll punish you with one hour of flogging."

"Sir," says one of the judge's assistants quietly, "this man can't hear."

But the judge does not hear his assistant's words. He can only imagine what the man has said.

"Ah! I didn't know that," he shouts. "Flog this terrible criminal for *two* hours!"

That afternoon, crowds of people hurry to the Place de Grève for the flogging of the famous bellringer. A Parisian woman, Madame Oudarde Musnier, is taking her friend and the friend's young son there. They have also brought a cake for Sachette, the poor woman in the Tower of Roland.

ESL CENTER

"Let's hurry, Mahiette," says Oudarde Musnier to her guest. "We don't want to miss the flogging."

"There's a crowd near the bridge. Is that the place?" asks Mahiette. This is her first trip to Paris.

"No, listen," Oudarde says. "That's little Esmeralda, the gypsy. Come and see her. She sings beautifully and she's the best dancer in Paris."

"No, we can't go near her," says Mahiette. "She'll steal my son. Don't you know the story of Pâquette la Chantefleurie?"

"No, please tell me about her."

"Pâquette la Chantefleurie was a pretty girl from Rheims, my hometown. As children, we went to the same school and often played together. When we were only fourteen years old, Pâquette came to school with something new. She was wearing a beautiful gold cross around her neck. The next day, she was wearing a pretty new dress. Her father was dead and her mother had very little money. We knew that the new things were from a man. Pâquette sold her body for these nice gifts.

"Then her mother died. Pâquette was alone and had to make her living on the streets. By the age of twenty, she looked old and sad. But then the best thing happened to her. She had a beautiful baby girl, and she became beautiful again, too. At last, she had someone to love. She was a wonderful mother."

"How did they live?" Oudarde asks.

"Pâquette had to sell herself again, but she was happy. She used all of her money to buy things for Agnès, her baby. Agnès had the most beautiful clothes and even a little pair of pink shoes. I saw the baby once. She had golden skin and big black eyes and black hair. She was a happy baby, too, and her mother loved her more every day."

"It's a good story," says Oudarde as the women walk along. "But you haven't explained about the gypsies."

"One day, a group of gypsies came to Rheims. People were

afraid of them because they seemed different, maybe even dangerous. They could look at a person's hand and read the future. Pâquette took Agnès to the gypsies and asked about the baby's future."

"What did they tell her?"

"One old gypsy said, 'She'll be a queen.' So Pâquette felt happy and wanted to tell someone about Agnès's good luck. When the baby was asleep, she hurried to a neighbor's house."

"What happened?"

"While Pâquette was out, the gypsies broke into her little house. They stole Agnès. Some people saw them with the baby, but the gypsies quickly disappeared into the night. They left a little boy in Agnès's bed. He was about four years old, and the poor thing was an ugly hunchback with bright red hair and only one eye. Pâquette screamed and cried, and a neighbor took the boy away. Nobody knows what happened to him."

"But what happened to Pâquette and her baby?" asks Oudarde.

"Pâquette found one of Agnès's pink shoes on the floor. She searched for the gypsies, but they were gone. Her hair turned gray during the night, and she disappeared from Rheims. Now do you understand why I don't want my child near any gypsies?" asks Mahiette.

"Yes, of course," says Oudarde. "But, look, here we are at the Tower of Roland. The cake is for Sachette, another poor, unhappy woman."

The two women look through the window of Sachette's prison. Sachette is silent. She is very pale and thin and has long gray hair. She is looking at something in the corner of the small, dark room and does not notice the women.

"This is strange," says Mahiette. Tears are running down her face. "What's the witch's name?" she asks her friend.

"We call her Sachette."

"And I," says Mahiette, "call her Pâquette la Chantefleurie. Look in the corner." Oudarde looks and sees a pink baby's shoe. Then she begins to cry, too.

The two women leave the cake for Sachette and hurry to the Place de Grève. They wait patiently with a large crowd of people until the prisoner, Quasimodo, arrives. Is the Hunchback of Notre-Dame the boy that the gypsies left in Agnès's bed sixteen years ago? Yesterday, he was the people's Pope of Fools and enjoyed his special day. Today, his hands and feet are tied and he waits for the King's torturer, Pierrat Torterue. When Torterue is ready, Quasimodo is tied to the great wooden wheel. The flogging begins when the church bell rings the hour.

The wheel turns and the torturer hits Quasimodo's back and shoulders with his short rope. Quasimodo jumps like a person surprised in his sleep. He tries to free himself, but he is tied too tightly to the wheel. The wheel continues to turn, and Torterue hits the hunchback again and again. Soon blood is running down Quasimodo's back, and drops of it are flying into the air.

Quasimodo is quiet now and does not move. He does not understand why this is happening to him. Finally, the hour has ended and the torturer stops. His two assistants wash the blood from Quasimodo's back.

But Quasimodo's suffering has not ended. While he waits for his second hour of flogging, the people in the crowd shout at him. He cannot hear their words, but he can see their ugly faces. Then they begin to throw stones at him. Quasimodo stays quiet, but his face is red and angry.

Suddenly, he sees the one person who can help him. Quasimodo smiles sweetly because Father Claude Frollo is walking through the crowd. The priest comes near and his eyes meet Quasimodo's happy face. But Father Claude neither stops nor speaks. He looks at the ground and hurries away, and Quasimodo's smile disappears.

The second hour of flogging begins. Again, Quasimodo tries to free himself from the wheel, and the crowd shouts and laughs.

Oudarde looks and sees a pink baby's shoe.

fter a few terrible minutes, the hunchback looks at the crowd and cries painfully, "Some water!" But the people do not help the hunchback.

Again, Quasimodo cries, "Some water!" Everybody laughs.

Then a young girl with a little white goat pushes through the crowd. Quasimodo sees the gypsy girl from the night before. He thinks that she, too, wants to punish him.

Without a word, Esmeralda climbs up to Quasimodo. She kindly lifts a cup of water to his mouth and he drinks. A big tear slowly falls from his only eye. Enjoying this beautiful picture, the people are silent now. But one voice calls out loudly and clearly. Through her window, Sachette, the witch in the Tower of Roland, has seen Esmeralda.

"Go away, gypsy!" Sachette screams. "Thief! Thief!"

Chapter 3   Evil Thoughts and Evil Actions

It is a fine day at the beginning of March, two months after Quasimodo's flogging in the Place de Grève. Opposite the great Cathedral of Notre-Dame, there is a large house. It is owned by the Gondelauriers, one of the richest families in Paris. On this beautiful afternoon, Mademoiselle Fleur-de-Lys de Gondelaurier is sitting in the front yard with a group of her friends. They are busy, cutting cloth and telling stories. These girls are all young, pretty, and very rich. They live comfortable lives in expensive houses, with beautiful furniture and delicious food.

Fleur-de-Lys has a special visitor: Phoebus de Châteaupers, officer of the King's Guard and her future husband. The officer is happy that Fleur-de-Lys is pretty and rich. He is bored, though, in her company. He wants to be in a cheap bar with his soldier friends, talking to the girls there. But for now, he tries to talk to his future wife.

20

"My dear," he says to Fleur-de-Lys, "what are you making?"

"It's a birthday gift for my mother, as I told you ten minutes ago," answers Fleur-de-Lys coldly. She knows that the handsome officer is bored with her.

Suddenly, Bérangère, Fleur-de-Lys's little sister, calls everyone to the gate. "Look at that pretty girl. She dances very well and she has a little goat with her."

The officer does not look bored now. In fact, he is very interested in what he sees.

"Phoebus," says Fleur-de-Lys, "didn't you save a gypsy girl from the hands of thieves about two months ago?"

"You're right. I believe I did," the officer answers.

"Is that your gypsy girl in front of the cathedral?" Fleur-de-Lys asks.

"I think you're correct. She had a little goat with her."

"Look in the tower, near the top of the cathedral, sister," says Bérangère. "Who is that man in black up there?"

All the young ladies look up and see a priest at one of the high windows in the tower. His eyes are on the dancing girl.

"It's Father Claude Frollo," says Fleur-de-Lys. "He hates gypsy girls. Why is he watching her so carefully?"

"She dances beautifully," says one of Fleur-de-Lys's friends.

"Phoebus, since you know the girl, ask her to dance for us," orders Fleur-de-Lys.

Phoebus invites Esmeralda to the house and soon she is dancing for the party of young ladies. As Fleur-de-Lys and her friends watch, they each have one thought: She is surely the most beautiful girl in Paris. The girls do not want to be polite to Esmeralda. But Phoebus is clearly interested in her.

"My pretty child," Phoebus says after Esmeralda's dance, "we met in January. Do you remember me?"

Esmeralda says, "Oh, yes." She forgets about the other people in the yard. She looks into the officer's eyes and smiles sweetly.

"Please, tell me your name," the officer says quietly.

"Esmeralda," the girl answers.

The young ladies laugh at this strange name, but Phoebus notices only Esmeralda.

"Monsieur Torterue gave that ugly hunchback a good flogging. I hope you aren't afraid now in the streets at night."

"No, sir," Esmeralda says, smiling at Phoebus. She looks more beautiful than ever.

"Call for me if you are. I will help you, day or night," Phoebus says bravely.

"You seem happy with this gypsy girl," says Fleur-de-Lys.

"And why not?" asks Phoebus.

The other young ladies laugh at these words. But Fleur-de-Lys turns her face away from Phoebus as her eyes fill with tears.

Bérangère calls, "Sister, come and see the goat's trick." The little girl has been in a corner of the yard, playing with Djali. Around its neck, the goat always carries a little bag of letters on pieces of wood. Bérangère has thrown the letters on the ground and the goat has made a word with them.

The young ladies hurry over to look at the little goat's trick.

"Did the goat do that?" asks Fleur-de-Lys when she sees the word on the ground.

"Yes, sister."

The letters spell P H O E B U S.

"The goat has written your name, Phoebus!" cries one of the young ladies to the officer. "She's a witch."

"You have a wonderful memory," Fleur-de-Lys says to Esmeralda. Then she begins to cry and hurries through a door into the house.

"Leave us immediately, gypsy witch," shouts one of Fleur-de-Lys's friends.

Esmeralda hurries through the gate into the street, followed by Djali.

"The goat has written your name, Phoebus!"

Phoebus de Châteaupers stands alone in the yard. He stops and thinks, then he follows the gypsy girl.

◆

Father Claude Frollo heard Esmeralda's music in the square before she and her goat disappeared into the Gondelauriers' yard. He went to a high window in a tower in the cathedral and, as usual, watched the gypsy girl with great interest. On this morning, he also noticed a young man with her. The priest hurried down the stairs. Esmeralda was gone, but now he saw the young man's face clearly.

"Pierre Gringoire!" Claude Frollo said. "What are you doing here? You haven't been in church for months. Why are you going around with that gypsy girl?"

"For the very good reason that she's my wife and I'm her husband," answered Pierre Gringoire.

The priest's eyes turned to fire. "Are you really her husband? Have you touched her? Has *any* man touched her?"

"Please, calm down. Neither I nor any other man has touched the beautiful Esmeralda." Gringoire told the priest about his strange wedding in the City of Thieves.

"My wife," the writer continued, "never knew her mother or her father. She wears a little bag tied around her neck. It holds a secret, and it will help her find her parents one day. But the secret will not help her if she sleeps with a man."

"Are you sure that she has never known a man?" the priest asked. His eyes were wild and his voice was deep and quiet.

"Esmeralda is good, like a child. She believes that the world is good, too. She loves her gypsy friends, her music, and Djali, her goat. She's afraid of only two people. First, there's Sachette, the witch who hates gypsy women. She shouts at Esmeralda when she's near the Tower of Roland. And, second, there's a terrible priest who watches her all the time."

24

"And you? Do you love her?" asked Father Claude.

"She's very kind to me. She gives me a place to sleep and food every day. And have you seen Djali? She's the most wonderful goat in the world. *She* loves me, and I love her. She can tell the time and the date, and now she can spell. My wife gives her letters, and she spells *Phoebus*."

"Phoebus?" asked the priest. "Why Phoebus?"

"It's a mystery to me," answered Gringoire. "But Esmeralda often says this word quietly to herself."

"Listen, Pierre," said the priest before returning to the cathedral, "don't touch that girl. She's dangerous."

♦

A few days later, Father Claude Frollo is walking through one of the noisy squares near the cathedral in the late afternoon. As usual, he is wearing his long black coat, closed tightly around his neck, and he is studying the ground. He looks up suddenly when he hears loud voices and the name *Phoebus*.

"Phoebus, my good man, tell us more about this gypsy girl," shouts a man.

A group of soldiers is drinking inside a dark bar.

Officer Phoebus de Châteaupers laughs and says, "I can't tell you very much now. She's very beautiful and has a little white goat. I'm meeting her at seven o'clock. After tonight, I'll tell you everything about her."

The soldiers laugh and buy Phoebus another drink. Claude Frollo's eyes burn with an angry fire. He hides in the shadows outside the bar and waits for Phoebus de Châteaupers.

At six thirty, the soldiers push their officer out the door. "Good luck! Tell us everything tomorrow!" they shout.

After a block or two, Phoebus notices that someone is following him. There is a shadow moving along the walls. He stops. The shadow stops. He continues. The shadow continues, too. Phoebus is not afraid. He is young and strong, and he has had a lot to drink. He calls to the stranger.

"Sir, if you are a thief, go home. I don't have any money."

"Officer Phoebus de Châteaupers, I don't want your money. I know you're going to meet a girl at seven o'clock," the mystery man in the long black coat says.

"How do you know my name and my plans? Are you a sorcerer?" Phoebus asks. Then he takes out his knife and says, "Leave or fight."

"Sir," says the priest, "have you forgotten your meeting with the beautiful gypsy girl? We can fight tomorrow, or next week. But first, meet your girl."

Phoebus is really quite a stupid young man and quickly forgets about fighting. "You're very kind, sir," he says. "I don't want to miss this girl. Goodbye."

"Wait! Where are you going to meet her?" asks the priest.

"On the Saint-Michel bridge, then I'll take her to a small hotel. I can pay the old woman for an hour for one of her dirty little rooms." Then Phoebus checks his pockets. "Oh, no. I've spent my last penny."

"I'll give you the money," the priest says, "if you do something for me."

"What do you want?" Phoebus asks.

"I'm looking for a gypsy girl. I want to hide in the hotel room and see your girl. Maybe she's the one I'm looking for," explains the priest.

"All right. Give me the money and we'll be friends for tonight," agrees Phoebus.

The men go to Madame Falourdel's small hotel and pay for a room. The priest hides in the closet and waits.

Soon the door opens and the two young people walk in. Father Claude watches everything through a hole in the rough closet door. The picture in front of him makes his heart burn.

Phoebus sits next to Esmeralda on an old sofa near a broken window. The river runs below the window. The soldier looks very handsome in his fine clothes. Esmeralda is nervous and very excited about this meeting.

"At last we're alone, my pretty one," says Phoebus.

"Are you happy with me?" asks the girl.

"Of course!" says Phoebus. "You're wonderful!"

"No, I'm not. I will break a promise tonight," says Esmeralda. She touches the little bag she wears around her neck. "But if I have you, I won't need a mother or a father."

"I don't understand you," Phoebus says.

"Oh, sir, I love you! You saved my life. You're good and brave and strong. I love your name, too. My dear Phoebus, do you love me?" asks the girl.

"Of course I love you, dear girl. My body, my heart, my blood— all belong to you. I have loved nobody except you." Phoebus says these words very easily because he has said them to many girls before. But Esmeralda believes every word.

"I want to die at this minute," she says.

Phoebus sees how happy she is. He steals a kiss.

"Die!" he cries. "No, Esmenarda... excuse me, your name is difficult for me. No—now is the time to live!"

As he talks about his love for her, Phoebus tries to take off Esmeralda's belt and then her little jacket.

"What are you doing?" she asks him.

"You're with me now. You don't need these strange gypsy clothes," says Phoebus.

"I'm with you," says Esmeralda dreamily. She touches the little bag at her neck and says, "Take all of me. I'm yours."

Phoebus puts his arm around her waist and kisses her again.

The priest can see Esmeralda's beautiful shoulders and he can see the light of love in her eyes. He has never touched a woman, and this is making him crazy.

Suddenly, above Phoebus's head, Esmeralda sees an angry face. It is the priest who always follows her. In his hand is a knife and he pushes it into Phoebus's neck. Esmeralda's eyes close, and she falls to the floor. But just before everything goes black, she feels a terrible burning kiss on her mouth.

When Esmeralda wakes up, the little room is full of soldiers from the King's Guard. The window is open and the priest has disappeared. The soldiers carry Phoebus's bloody body down the stairs. One of them looks back at Esmeralda and says, "There's the witch who did this to Officer Phoebus."

Chapter 4   One Honest Heart

It is now May and nobody in the City of Thieves has seen Esmeralda and her little goat for more than a month. The gypsies are worried, and Pierre Gringoire is, too. One morning he is walking past the Tournelle, a prison for criminals, when he sees a large crowd at the gates.

"What's happening?" he asks a young man in the crowd.

"There's a woman in court today. They say she murdered an officer of the King's Guard. Some people say she's a witch."

Pierre Gringoire has always enjoyed listening to judges and lawyers, so he follows the crowd into the courtroom. He is pleased to see a large group of lawyers at a big table with piles of papers around them. Their chief is Monsieur Jacques Charmolue, the King's lawyer, and the main judge is Robert d'Estouteville.

"Who's the criminal?" Gringoire asks his neighbor.

"It's a woman, sir. You can't see her face from here."

"Silence!" shouts the officer of the court. "Madame Falourdel will now speak to the court."

"Judge, sir," the poor old woman begins, "I'm an honest woman. I own a small hotel—it's my house, also—on the Saint-Michel

Suddenly, above Phoebus's head, Esmeralda sees an angry face.

bridge. I've done nothing wrong, but evil things happened in my house on the night of March 29."

"Please, tell the court," orders Judge d'Estouteville.

"Two men knocked at my door. A young, handsome soldier and a man in a long black coat and hat. I couldn't see his face. The soldier paid me for my best room at the top of the house. Then the two men climbed the stairs. Soon the soldier came down again and left. He returned with a pretty gypsy girl and a goat.

"After about half an hour I heard a terrible scream. Something fell on the floor above me and the window up there opened. I ran to my window and looked out. I saw the man in black drop from the window into the river below. The moon was very bright and I saw him clearly. He was wearing a priest's clothes. He swam toward the city."

"And what did you do?"

"I shouted for the King's Guard. When they came, I followed them upstairs. There was blood everywhere. The handsome soldier was lying on the floor with a knife in his neck. The girl wasn't hurt. She was lying on the floor with her clothes half on and half off. The guards found a knife in her pocket."

"Madame Falourdel," the judge says, "do you have anything more to tell us?"

"I think the priest and the girl were working together," says the old woman. "They planned to rob the handsome soldier. I think she's a witch and he's a sorcerer."

"Enough," says the judge. "*We* will decide that."

"Judge d'Estouteville," Monsieur Charmolue begins, "we talked to Officer Phoebus de Châteaupers in the hospital. He didn't know the man in black until the night at Madame Falourdel's hotel. This mysterious man, possibly an evil priest, gave the soldier the money for the hotel room. It was a trick."

The prisoner hears the name *Phoebus* and seems awake for the first time. "Phoebus!" she cries. "Where is he? Is he alive?"

"Woman, be silent," orders the judge. "That's not our business. He's dying. Now, please, be quiet."

Pierre Gringoire cannot believe his ears. He realizes now that the prisoner is his wife.

The judge turns to Esmeralda. "Girl, you're a gypsy. You know about evil ways. On the night of March 29, did you murder Phoebus de Châteaupers, officer of the King's Guard?"

"No, never. I love Phoebus. I didn't hurt him."

"Then explain the facts," says the judge.

"I did nothing wrong. It was that terrible priest. He follows me everywhere. I'm only a poor girl," Esmeralda says.

"A *gypsy* girl," says the judge.

"Judge," Monsieur Charmolue says, "she isn't honest. I suggest torture. That will give us the true story."

"Yes," the judge agrees. "Take her to the King's torturer. This court is closed for today."

The guards guide Esmeralda down many dark stairs to the torture room below the courthouse. There is a large open oven at one end of the room. The torturer, Monsieur Pierrat Torterue, keeps his tools red hot in this fire.

Esmeralda has tried to be brave during her walk from the courtroom, but now she is nervous. She sees the smiling, ugly face of the King's torturer. She also sees Monsieur Charmolue. He is sitting at a long desk with lawyers to his right and priests to his left.

"My dear child," says Monsieur Charmolue, "I will repeat my question. Did you murder Phoebus de Châteaupers, officer of the King's Guard, on the night of March 29?"

"No, sir. I love Phoebus."

"If that is your answer, Monsieur Torterue will have to do his job. Put her on the table," orders Monsieur Charmolue.

Esmeralda begins to shake with fear. Two guards lift her and tie her to the torture table. Esmeralda looks wildly around the room. Will nobody help her?

The guards roughly take off the girl's right shoe and sock. They place an ugly-looking tool on her pretty foot and begin to turn it.

"Oh, my Phoebus!" cries Esmeralda in a quiet, weak voice.

She sees Monsieur Torterue coming near the table with another tool, this time hot from the fire. Fear makes her strong, and she shouts, "Stop! Please, stop!"

Monsieur Charmolue holds his hand up and asks his question again. "Did you kill Phoebus de Châteaupers?"

"I did not, good sir."

"Continue the torture!"

The guards turn the tool on her foot again. The pain is very bad. Her foot is ready to break.

"Wait!" screams Esmeralda.

"Are you the murderer?" asks Charmolue again.

"Yes," cries the poor child. She cannot be brave. The torture is too terrible.

"Then you must die."

"Yes, I want death." Esmeralda falls back on to the table.

Jacques Charmolue turns to the lawyers and says, "Write it down. We now have the gypsy girl's true story. She's a murderer and a witch. She's in the service of the devil. This is true, isn't it?" he asks Esmeralda.

"Yes," she answers weakly. She has stopped fighting.

"Take her back to the judge," orders Charmolue.

In the crowded courtroom, Judge d'Estouteville hears Monsieur Charmolue's report. Then the judge says, "Gypsy girl, we find that you're a murderer and a witch. In two weeks' time you'll go to the Cathedral of Notre-Dame and prepare yourself for death. Then at noon on that day, we will hang you and your goat in the Place de Grève for your crimes."

Esmeralda is thrown into a wet, dark prison. She is completely alone. The only sound is cold water dropping into a dirty pool at her feet.

The pain is very bad.

Finally, one day or night—they are the same to Esmeralda—she hears a noise at the heavy door. She looks up, and the light hurts her eyes. She sees a man come through the door. He is dressed in black. Esmeralda cannot see his hands or face.

After a long silence, the girl says, "Who are you?"

"A priest."

At the sound of this voice, Esmeralda shakes with fear.

"Are you prepared?" the priest asks.

"For what?"

"For death. It will be tomorrow. Do you understand why you are here?"

"I did once, but now I don't." The girl begins to cry. "Sir, I'm cold and afraid. This is no life without light, without fire, without friends."

"Follow me," says the man. He touches the girl's arm.

"Oh, it's the icy hand of death. Who are you?" Esmeralda asks.

The priest takes his hat off and the girl sees Father Claude Frollo. She saw this face in Madame Falourdel's dirty little hotel above Phoebus's head. She remembers his burning kiss. This man killed Phoebus and he wants to kill her.

"It's you! The evil priest. Why do you follow me? You've tortured me, and you've killed my Phoebus. Why do you hate me?" Esmeralda asks.

"I cannot hate you. I love you!" cries the priest.

"What kind of love is this?" the girl shouts.

"It's a painful, secret love. It has destroyed my life. Before I met you, I was happy."

"And I was, too!" says Esmeralda.

"Quiet! I must tell my story. I was a good priest, an honest man. I was proud. I walked through the streets of Paris with my head high. I had religion and science, and those were enough. But then one day, when I was in my tower, I heard your music in the square below. I looked out and saw you—the most beautiful thing in the

34

world. I watched, and I was lost. My books held no interest. The cathedral became a prison. I wanted only to see you, to touch you, to love you.

"From that day, I was a different man. When I opened a book, I saw your face. I went into the cathedral, and I heard your voice. I followed you because I cannot live without you. I waited for you on street corners. I watched you from the top of my tower. Every day I became crazier with the idea of you in my head.

"Then one day I heard that soldier say your name. He laughed and joked about you. I followed him, and you know the rest."

"Oh, my Phoebus!" Esmeralda cries softly.

"Don't say that name. He didn't love you. He didn't even know your name. Look at me! I was with you in the courtroom. I saw you on the torturer's table. You suffered, but do you understand *my* torture? I watched you smile at that stupid soldier in that dirty room. I watched him touch you and kiss you. He wanted to use you and throw you away. But I love you and I can help you. They'll hang you tomorrow, but I can stop them. You can live. Touch my hand. Follow me out of this prison. Learn to love me. Learn to forgive me. Please! Please!"

Esmeralda looks into the priest's eyes and says, "What has happened to my Phoebus?"

"He's dead!" cries the priest.

"Dead!" Esmeralda says. She feels even colder now. "Then do not talk to me about living."

The priest is not listening. "The knife went deep," he says quietly to himself. "He's surely dead."

"Go! Leave, murderer! Love you? Forgive you? Never! My blood and the blood of Phoebus de Châteaupers are on your hands. You're a devil!" Esmeralda screams.

She falls to the floor. Father Claude takes his light, slowly climbs the stairs, and shuts the door. The room is black again.

♦

But the handsome officer is not dead. Phoebus de Châteaupers left the hospital after a few weeks. Nobody thought this information was important to the court. Phoebus quickly forgot about Esmeralda. In fact, on the day of her hanging, he is in Paris again. He is at the Gondelauriers' house, enjoying the conversation of Mademoiselle Fleur-de-Lys.

"Where have you been for two months?" the young lady asks.

"I'm a soldier," answers Phoebus. "I work for my king. We were at Queue-en-Brie. Look, what's happening in the square?" He does not want to answer any more questions.

The young lovers stand at the big open window and look across the square at the Cathedral of Notre-Dame.

"They are going to hang a witch at noon. She's preparing herself at the church," Fleur-de-Lys explains.

"What has she done?" asks Phoebus.

"I don't know. Listen, Phoebus. We're getting married soon. Have you ever loved another woman?" asks Fleur-de-Lys.

"My dear, of course not," Phoebus lies. "You're my one true love." Even he believes his own words at that minute. But then he sees Esmeralda outside the church, on her knees. "Let's go into the other room and talk to your mother," he suggests.

"No," says Fleur-de-Lys, "I want to watch."

Esmeralda is at the front of the cathedral. She is wearing a simple white dress and no shoes. Her beautiful black hair falls over her shoulders and around her neck is the little bag with her secret inside.

The priests carry the cross to Esmeralda, but she does not look up. One priest goes near her and puts his mouth very close to her ear.

"Will you have me?" the priest asks. Only the girl can hear his words. "I can save you right now."

Esmeralda looks at him and says, "You're a devil. Go away or I'll tell everyone your story."

Father Claude smiles a terrible smile. "They will not believe you. But answer me quickly. Will you have me?"

"Where's my Phoebus?"

"He's dead!" answers the priest. But he looks up at that minute and sees Phoebus de Châteaupers at the window of the Gondelauriers' great house. He cannot believe his eyes. "Die then! Nobody will have you!"

Claude Frollo turns his back on the girl and returns to the cathedral with the other priests.

After the doors of the cathedral close, the guards move toward the girl. Suddenly, Esmeralda looks up and cries happily, "Phoebus!" She, too, has seen him at the window. He is alive! The judge and the priest lied to her!

Esmeralda's eyes meet the officer's eyes. His handsome face changes when he sees her. He takes Fleur-de-Lys by the arm and quickly moves away from the window.

Esmeralda understands everything. She is going to die for the murder of Phoebus de Châteaupers. But he is alive! And he does not love her. He does not want to know her or help her.

Everyone is looking at the girl. They have not noticed a man in one of the lower towers of the cathedral. He has seen everything. As the guards pull Esmeralda away from the church, this man jumps to the ground. He knocks down the guards, and with one hand he picks up Esmeralda. He carries her over his shoulder and runs inside the church. A little goat runs out from the crowd and follows them. In a loud voice, the man cries, "Sanctuary!" Esmeralda is safe.

The crowd is silent. Then everyone shouts, "Sanctuary! Sanctuary!" They wanted a hanging, but now they are happy for Esmeralda. Nobody can touch her inside the walls of Notre-Dame.

Inside the church, Esmeralda sees that her friend, her helper, is Quasimodo, the hunchback. But now he is not ugly. To Esmeralda, and to the crowd outside, he is brave and good—the best man in

Paris on this day. The people watch him carry the girl to the top of the cathedral. Each time they see him run past one of the church windows, they shout, "Sanctuary! Sanctuary!"

In the cathedral, Quasimodo looks after Esmeralda. He gives her his own bed and his own food. He brings her warm clothes, and she has Djali with her for company. She is safe, but she cannot leave the cathedral. If she does, the guards will take her to the Place de Grève and hang her.

Father Claude Frollo did not see Quasimodo save Esmeralda. After his last private conversation with the girl at the door of the cathedral, he suffered more than ever. He left the city and walked through the fields, thinking about his lost love. He imagined the guards taking Esmeralda to her death in the Place de Grève. It is after noon now, the hour of her hanging. His only love, the only important person in his world is dead. Why did he destroy her? Why did his love for her drive him crazy?

The priest returns to Paris and to Notre-Dame at midnight. He falls to his knees and thinks of Esmeralda, now dead and cold in the ground. At last, he gets up and begins to climb the steps to his tower.

Suddenly, the priest feels a cold wind. He turns and looks into a dark corner. There he sees a sad woman in a long white dress with a white goat next to her. It is Esmeralda! "She's free," thinks Father Claude. "She's dead." He does not speak and the girl disappears without seeing him.

Next morning, Esmeralda's first in the cathedral, the sun is shining, and for the first time in months she is not afraid. Then she sees a terrible face at her door, and she turns her head away.

"Don't be afraid. I'm your friend," Quasimodo says. "I'll stand behind the wall. I don't want to scare you."

The voice is rough, but it is also kind. Esmeralda goes to the door and softly says, "Come here." She touches his arm and he looks up at her. She wants him to stay and to talk.

Esmeralda goes to the door and softly says, "Come here."

ESL CENTER

"I'm sorry," Quasimodo says. "I cannot hear you."

The girl looks at his ugly face and body. She is sad for him, but she is beginning to like him.

"Why did you save me?" she asks.

Quasimodo watches her mouth carefully. "I understand," he answers. "You're asking me why I saved you. Don't you remember? One night in January, I tried to carry you off. That was wrong, very wrong. But the next day, I was tied to the torturer's wheel. You brought water to me. You were my only friend. Now I'll help you if I can."

"You saved my life!" Esmeralda says and smiles at him. "We'll always be friends."

"I have something for you," says Quasimodo happily. "I cannot be near your room all the time. But take this whistle. If you need me, whistle for me. I can hear that."

The long days pass slowly for Esmeralda. Father Claude Frollo, of course, learns that she is not dead. She has found sanctuary in his cathedral. His mind cannot rest, and he walks through the dark, silent church for hours each night.

One night, the priest cannot stop himself, so he climbs to Esmeralda's little room. He steps across something at her door and silently goes in. Then he hurries to her bed and takes her in his arms.

Esmeralda sits up and tries to push the priest away. "Go away! Devil! Murderer!" she screams with hate.

"Please, please! Love me!" the priest shouts. He kisses her neck and shoulders. "I need you. I can't live without you."

"Let me go!" cries Esmeralda. She tries to escape.

But the priest holds her down and shouts, "Be quiet! I'll have you!"

Esmeralda reaches out, finds Quasimodo's whistle on the floor, and puts it to her mouth. It makes a loud, clear sound.

"What's that?" asks the priest.

Suddenly, the priest is lifted up and thrown to the floor outside Esmeralda's room. As usual Quasimodo was sleeping at her door. He lifts a large knife above his head to kill this evil attacker. But the light from the moon shows Quasimodo the face of Father Claude Frollo. The hunchback drops the knife, but stands between him and Esmeralda.

"Father Claude, I will not hurt you. But you'll have to kill me before you touch this girl."

The priest runs down the stairs. His only thought is, "She loves Quasimodo and he defends her. But nobody will have her if I can't."

Chapter 5   Together in Death

Pierre Gringoire, the poor writer, has continued to live near the City of Thieves in Esmeralda's little house. He has heard that his wife is now safe in Notre-Dame. He is quite happy to live without her. In fact, he has begun to forget about Esmeralda, but sometimes he thinks about Djali, his little friend.

One afternoon, Gringoire is walking near the river when he feels a hand on his shoulder.

"Monsieur Gringoire, how are you?" asks Father Claude Frollo.

"I'm very well, Father," answers Gringoire. "My health is not excellent—but good."

He is surprised by the changes in the priest. The older man's hair is almost white now, his skin is very pale, and his eyes are deep in his head.

"Then you have no problems?" asks the priest.

"No, not I."

"But you are still poor?"

"Poor, yes, but not unhappy."

"And what about your pretty wife?" asks the priest.

"I'm sorry, I don't have any information about her. Isn't she in your cathedral?" asks Gringoire.

"Yes, that's correct. But Judge Robert d'Estouteville has ordered the King's Guard to get her out of the church. She'll be hanged in three days. She saved your life. Don't you want to help her?" asks the priest.

"It's true—she did save my life," says the writer. "But there's nothing I can do for her. I don't want them to hang me, too."

"You're friends with the thieves and gypsies. Can't they help?" suggests the priest.

He clearly has an idea in his head, but Pierre Gringoire does not notice this.

Gringoire stops and thinks for a minute. "Yes . . . they're fine people and they love Esmeralda. Maybe they can attack the cathedral and save her. And the goat, of course. I'll ask them to do it tomorrow evening. It's a good plan, isn't it?"

"A very good plan, but listen to me," the priest says coldly. "Find out everything about the attack and come to me tomorrow with this information. You aren't a soldier. But while they're fighting, you and I will help your poor wife."

That evening, Pierre Gringoire meets with the King of Thieves and tells him about his plan. The king is happy to help Esmeralda, and to help himself, too. If the thieves get inside the old church at night, they will not only find the girl, but also the cathedral's gold and silver. The thieves and gypsies quickly prepare for the attack.

At midnight on the following day, the King of Thieves calls his people together. "Our sister, Esmeralda, is alive and safe, but in the morning the King's Guard will come for her. They want to hang her tomorrow at noon in the Place de Grève. Follow me and we'll save her!"

A great crowd of thieves and gypsies follow the king silently through the dark streets of the capital to Notre-Dame. They are carrying knives, sticks, and all kinds of tools.

At the same time, Quasimodo is walking through the great church. He cannot sleep. He has locked the big door and has checked every corner of Notre-Dame. Esmeralda is sleeping safely in her little room, but the hunchback feels nervous for some reason. Is there a new danger in the world outside the cathedral? Will Father Claude try to hurt Esmeralda again?

Since his attack on Esmeralda, the priest has stayed away from the girl's little room. But he has acted badly toward Quasimodo. He has given him more work and sometimes he even hits him. Quasimodo is patient and follows the priest's orders. He will not make any trouble for Father Claude, but he watches him. The hunchback will stop him if he goes near Esmeralda. But the priest has not been near her room again.

Quasimodo climbs to the top of the north tower as the party of thieves and gypsies comes closer. With his one good eye, he sees them moving toward Notre-Dame. The bellringer is afraid now. Why are they coming toward him and toward Esmeralda? He imagines that the people of Paris hate her as much as they hate him.

Quasimodo thinks quickly. He cannot escape from the church with the gypsy girl, so he will fight. Some workers have been in the south tower and he runs there. He will use their heavy tools, their wood, their stones, and their metal to stop his enemies.

He looks out and sees the crowd of people arrive at the great door.

"Our sister is not a murderer!" the King of Thieves shouts. "Give her to us or we will break the doors of this church. We will take her and your gold!"

Quasimodo cannot hear these words. He believes that these people are Esmeralda's enemies. When they attack the great doors, the hunchback begins to throw the heavy builders' material on their heads. He kills a great number of the thieves and gypsies, but they continue to fight. They find ladders and begin to climb up the sides of the church. But Quasimodo is as strong as a hundred men. He throws men off the building and pushes ladders into the square below. He pours red hot metal on their heads, but the gypsies and thieves continue to attack. Poor Quasimodo! He needs help. Suddenly, he sees soldiers on horses arriving at the square. The King's Guard, with Officer Phoebus de Châteaupers at the head, have come to stop the fight. The gypsies and thieves disappear down every narrow street near the cathedral, leaving a pile of dead bodies in the square.

Quasimodo cannot believe his luck. He falls to his knees and thanks God for this help. Esmeralda is safe again and he runs to her room. But when he gets to the girl's sanctuary, it is empty.

♦

When the King of Thieves and his men began their attack on the Cathedral of Notre-Dame, Esmeralda was sleeping. But the noise outside soon woke her. She ran to the window, and in the moonlight she saw the crowd of men. Some were trying to break down the doors of the church. Others were climbing the walls. The noise became louder and the gypsy girl was afraid. She believed that the men wanted to take her from the church. They wanted to hang her. She hurried back to her room and hid from these enemies.

As she shook with fear on her bed, Esmeralda heard the sound of footsteps coming toward her room. Suddenly, two men walked through her door. The girl cried out for help.

"Don't be afraid," said one of the men. "It's me, Pierre Gringoire, your husband and your friend."

Esmeralda was calmer when she heard this name. She looked up and saw the writer. But she also saw the other man behind Gringoire. He was dressed in black from head to toe and his face was covered.

"Who's that with you?" Esmeralda asked.

Quasimodo throws men off the building.

"Have no fear," answered Gringoire. "It's a friend of mine. We've come to save you. Follow us."

"Is that true?" the girl asked nervously.

"Yes, very true. Come quickly. There's danger outside," said Gringoire.

"I will," Esmeralda said, "but why doesn't your friend speak?"

"He is a great thinker, a serious man. Don't worry about him," Gringoire answered.

The writer took Esmeralda by the hand and they followed the man in black down the stairs of the tower, through the dark church to a small door. The man opened this door with a key, and the three people and the little goat were outside next to the river. Esmeralda sat near Gringoire and Djali as they moved silently across the water in a small boat. She was afraid of the man in black. She was also scared by the noise from Notre-Dame. "The gypsy!" the soldiers shouted. "The witch! Death for the gypsy girl!"

These voices scared Gringoire, too. He looked at Esmeralda and at Djali and thought, "I cannot save both of you."

When the boat reached the opposite side of the river, Gringoire jumped out and hurried into the dark night with Djali. Esmeralda was alone now with the terrible man in black. She tried to speak, to call for Gringoire. No sound came from her mouth. The man did not speak either. He took her roughly by the hand and pulled her quickly toward the Place de Grève.

Esmeralda looked around at the dark houses and the empty streets. The only sounds came from the cathedral across the river. "Death to the gypsy!" the voices shouted again and again. Esmeralda's hope was gone.

At the Place de Grève, she saw the place for hangings and she began to shake again. "Who are you?" she cried. "Why have you brought me here?"

The man stopped, turned to her, and uncovered his face.

"I knew it! You! The priest!" cried Esmeralda. "It's the end."

"This is the Place de Grève," the priest said. "It's time to decide. But don't talk to me of your Phoebus. Don't say his name." The priest walked up and down nervously. He held Esmeralda's hand tightly and pulled her along with him.

Then he stopped and said, "Look at me! The soldiers are searching for you. You can hear them. Judge d'Estouteville has given them orders. They will find you soon, bring you here, and hang you today at noon.

"Don't speak. Don't say a word. I love you. I can save you. Look at this place. Choose between me and the hangman."

Esmeralda pulled her hand away from the priest. "I choose death," she said to him. "You are worse than hanging to me."

"But I love you!" cried the priest. "I have lost everything because of you, but still you hate me."

Claude Frollo was crying now. He hung his head and tears ran down his sad face.

"Because of you. Because of you," he repeated quietly. Then he remembered where he was. "You've seen me cry, but you feel nothing for me. I don't want to see you die. Give me one kind word and I'll save you. Say you *want* to love me."

"You're a murderer," Esmeralda said coldly. "I belong to Phoebus. I love him. You're old and evil. Go away!"

"Die then!" the priest screamed. He shook her and threw her to the ground.

Then the priest called out in a loud voice, "Sachette! Sachette! Here's the gypsy girl. Take her and punish her." He pulled Esmeralda to the witch's prison in the Tower of Roland and pushed her against the window in the wall. A thin hand reached out and held the girl's pretty arm.

"Hold tight," ordered the priest. "I will bring the soldiers here. They will hang her at noon. It's finished."

The girl watched Father Claude Frollo hurry toward the river.

♦

Now, as the dark sky begins to lighten, Esmeralda sees the face of Sachette on the other side of the window. The witch's thin fingers hold Esmeralda's arm tightly and her eyes are full of hate for the gypsy. The girl falls against the wall. She knows that Sachette will never help her. She knows that this is the day of her death.

"What have I done to you?" she asks the old woman.

"You know your crime. I had a pretty little child, my Agnès," she begins. "Your people—the gypsies—stole her from me. They stole her and ate her. That's what you did to me."

"But maybe I wasn't born then," Esmeralda answers.

"Oh, yes. You were one of them. They came fifteen years ago to my little house in Rheims. Agnès was the most beautiful baby in the world. You took her and you took my life. Poor little child! Now I'll watch you hang."

There is more light in the sky now and Esmeralda hears the soldiers coming toward the Place de Grève.

"I've done nothing to you. Please don't hold me here. I don't want to die," says the girl.

"My Agnès didn't want to die!" screams Sachette. "Give me back my child and you can live. Look, this little shoe is the only thing that the gypsies left me."

"Show me that shoe!" cries Esmeralda. With her free hand she pulls the little bag from around her neck. She takes out a baby's shoe and a small note. It says, *When you find the other shoe, your mother will open her arms to you.*

Sachette's eyes grow wide. She looks at the shoe and reads the note. "My daughter! My daughter!" she cries.

"Mother!" answers Esmeralda.

The witch opens the door and pulls the girl into her dark prison. Then she kisses Esmeralda's hands and holds her in her arms. The tears of fifteen years run down her face, but now they are tears of happiness.

"My child, my daughter," she repeats again and again. "How

beautiful you are! We'll leave here and return to Rheims. We'll be happy again. I'll love you and protect you."

"Mother!" says Esmeralda. "I'm so happy!"

Suddenly, the two women hear the sound of horses. Esmeralda throws her arms around Sachette and cries, "Save me, Mother! They're coming for me. They want to kill me."

"They can't take you from me. I've only had you for a minute," cries Sachette. She looks out the window. "They're almost here. I'll talk to them. Hide in that corner. I'll say that you've escaped."

Esmeralda hurries to the dark corner and Sachette covers her with an old sheet and a big stone. Then she hears the voice of Father Claude Frollo as he passes her door. "This way, Officer Phoebus de Châteaupers!" the priest shouts.

Esmeralda hears this name and tries to move.

"Don't move!" orders Sachette.

A group of soldiers on horseback now arrive. Sachette stands in the door, so nobody can look inside.

"Old woman," says an officer, "we're looking for a young gypsy. The priest says you have her."

"I don't know anything about a gypsy. I hate all of them," says Sachette.

"He told us, 'The girl is with the witch,'" says one of the soldiers.

"She was here," Sachette says quickly, "but she bit me and ran away."

"Which way did she go?" asks the officer.

"Toward Mouton Street, I think," Sachette says.

"We've been on Mouton Street and we didn't see a gypsy girl."

"Maybe she went toward the river," says Sachette.

"Old woman, you're lying! Let's take her to the torturer and get the true story," shouts one of the soldiers.

"Yes, take me! Quick! Let's leave now," says the witch. She wants to guide the soldiers away from Esmeralda.

"She really is crazy," says one of the soldiers.

"She's lived here for fifteen years," the officer says. "She hates gypsy women. She can't help us. Let's go."

Sachette watches the soldiers return to their horses. She thinks her daughter will be safe. Now they will be happy together.

Then another officer arrives on horseback.

"Sir, gypsies are not my business. With your permission, I will return to my company." The voice belongs to Phoebus de Châteaupers, officer of the King's Guard.

Esmeralda hears the voice and lifts her head. Before her mother can stop her, the girl runs to the window.

"Phoebus! Here I am, my Phoebus!" she shouts.

Phoebus has already ridden off, so he does not hear Esmeralda's cry. But the other soldiers are still there.

"The witch was lying. I thought so," says the officer. "Take the girl away and hang her now. It's the King's order."

Sachette cannot speak. She puts her arms around her daughter's waist and holds tight.

"Mother! Protect me!" cries Esmeralda, as the soldiers pull the two women out of the prison.

The sun is climbing into the sky. There is nobody in the Place de Grève, but two men are watching this terrible picture. They are at the top of one of the towers of Notre-Dame, on the other side of the river.

The hangman is waiting for the girl with his rope as the soldiers carry her and her mother to his ladder. When Sachette sees the rope, she begins to cry. The soldiers pull her away and the hangman carries Esmeralda up the ladder.

"No! No! I don't want to die!" the girl screams.

The hangman, with tears in his eyes, places the rope around Esmeralda's beautiful neck. Sachette tries to climb the ladder. She tries to stop the hangman, but he pushes her to the ground. Sachette hits her head on the hard earth and dies immediately. Then the hangman finishes his job.

♦

Earlier at the cathedral, Esmeralda's empty room made Quasimodo crazy. Where was she? Was she in danger? The poor bellringer ran through the cathedral calling her name. When the soldiers arrived, he opened the big door for them. He did not realize that they, not the gypsies, were Esmeralda's enemies.

After searching every corner of the great church, the soldiers left. Quasimodo returned to Esmeralda's little room and tried to think. Who took Esmeralda? There was only one possible answer: Father Claude Frollo. He was the only person with a key to Esmeralda's room. The hunchback remembered the priest's attacks on the girl. But even now Quasimodo's love for Father Claude was very deep.

Quasimodo climbed to the top of Notre-Dame and saw Father Claude disappear behind the door of the north tower. From this tower, a person can see the Place de Grève. Fearful and angry, the hunchback silently followed the priest.

When he reached the tower, Quasimodo found Father Claude. He wanted to ask him about Esmeralda. But the priest was in another world. He did not hear or see the hunchback. He was watching something, and only this existed for him. Quasimodo stood behind him and followed his eyes to the Place de Grève.

A group of soldiers was in the square at the hanging place. A man was pulling something white along the ground, with something black on top of it. Suddenly the sun shone brightly and Quasimodo could see clearly. A soldier pulled a woman in black away from a girl in white. Then another man, the King's hangman, began to climb the ladder with the girl over his shoulder. There was a rope around her neck. The girl was his Esmeralda.

Claude Frollo climbed on to the wall that goes around the north tower. He wanted to see better. Suddenly, the hangman kicked the ladder away, and Esmeralda hung in the air at the end of the rope. Her body shook with terrible pain before her neck broke.

An evil laugh came from the priest. Quasimodo did not hear the laugh, but he saw it and ran toward the priest. With his two big hands, he pushed Claude Frollo over the side of the tower to his death a hundred meters below.

The poor bellringer looked again at Esmeralda's dead body, hanging from the rope. A river of tears fell from his single eye. Then he looked down at the body of Father Claude Frollo. "All that I ever loved!" he cried.

That same evening, Quasimodo disappeared and was never seen again. Stories about the Cathedral of Notre-Dame and the hunchback and the priest passed from person to person through Paris. Was Quasimodo the devil? Did he mysteriously carry his evil sorcerer, the real Claude Frollo, away in the night?

♦

The writer, Pierre Gringoire, returned to Esmeralda's little house and lived happily with Djali. He tried many different jobs and finally wrote another play. It was a success, and many more after it were successful, too. The writer's dream came true: he was rich and famous.

Phoebus de Châteaupers also became rich, but he did not live happily. He married Fleur-de-Lys de Gondelaurier.

After Esmeralda's death, her body was thrown into the ground with the bodies of other murderers killed by the state. About two years later, when another body was added to the pile, the police discovered something interesting in the ground. They found two skeletons: one was a woman with a little bag around her neck; the other, a man with a hump on his back and some red hair near his head. The male skeleton was holding the female in his arms. The man's neck was not broken by the hangman's rope. He took himself to this place and died there.

He pushed Claude Frollo over the side of the tower to his death a hundred meters below.

ACTIVITIES

Chapter 1

Before you read

1 Look at the picture on the front of the book. What can you see? Describe the picture.
2 Read the Introduction and answer these questions.
   a Who are the three most important people in the story?
   b What city do they live in?
   c What is Notre-Dame?
   d Which country was the writer from?
3 Look at the Word List at the back of the book.
   a What are the words in your language? Check new words in your dictionary.
   b Seven of the words can be words for people. What are they?

While you read

4 Who does these things? Write the letters for people's names.
   Pierre Gringoire (PG)   Quasimodo (Q)   Esmeralda (E)
   Claude Frollo (CF)   Sachette (S)   Phoebus de Châteaupers (PC)
   a He is made the Pope of Fools.   .....
   b She dances in the Place de Grève.   .....
   c She lives in the Tower of Roland near the Place de Grève.   .....
   d He says that Esmeralda is evil.   .....
   e He saves Esmeralda from Quasimodo in a dark street.   .....
   f He goes by accident into the City of Thieves.   .....

After you read

5 January 6, 1482 is a strange and exciting day, for Quasimodo. What happens to him? What does he do? Describe his day.
6 Discuss these questions.
   a At the end of the day, Esmeralda is married to Gringoire and in love with Phoebus. What does she know about these two men?
   b What is the City of Thieves? Who lives there? Who is the most important person there? What happens to visitors?

7 Imagine that you are Pierre Gringoire. On January 7, you meet a friend in a bar. He asks, "What happened to you after they stopped the play?" Tell him.

Chapter 2

Before you read

8 Discuss this question. You have met the three main people in the story—Quasimodo, Esmeralda, and Father Claude Frollo. At this point in the story, which of these three do you think are good, kind, beautiful, intelligent, sad, lonely, or evil?

While you read

9 Which is the right word?

   a As a young man, Frollo was unusually *intelligent / strong*.

   b After he becomes a bell ringer, Quasimodo can't *talk / hear*.

   c The people of Paris are *afraid of / sorry for* Quasimodo.

   d Quasimodo *hates / loves* Father Frollo.

   e As he grows older, Frollo becomes more and more *alone / religious*.

10 Complete each sentence with one word.

   a Quasimodo cannot .... the judge's questions.

   b Quasimodo is punished with .... hours of flogging.

   c Paquette's baby girl was stolen by the ....

   d There is a little pink .... in the corner of Sachette's room.

   e Esmeralda gives Quasimodo some ....

After you read

11 How do these people feel? Give reasons for your opinions.

   a Quasimodo, about Father Frollo

   b Father Frollo, about Quasimodo

   c Sachette, about Esmeralda

   d Esmeralda, about Sachette

12 Tell the story of Pâquette la Chantefleurie in your own words.

13 Remember your discussion of the three main people in the story, in Activity 8. Have you changed any of your opinions now?

Chapter 3

Before you read

14 Discuss these questions.

    a This chapter is called "Evil Thoughts and Evil Actions." Who will have evil thoughts? Who will do evil actions?

    b In this chapter, we meet Phoebus de Châteaupers, the handsome young officer, again. What do you remember about him? What kind of man is he?

While you read

15 Who:

    a is rich and beautiful? ....

    b is going to marry a girl only because she is rich? ....

    c watches Esmeralda all the time from the cathedral tower? ....

    d can spell the name PHOEBUS with wooden letters? ....

    e is living with Esmeralda and loves Djali? ....

    f has never known her parents? ....

16 Are these statements right (✓) or wrong (✗)?

    a Phoebus is going to meet Esmeralda at seven o'clock. .....

    b Frollo wants to fight Phoebus in the street. .....

    c Frollo hides in the closet in the hotel room. .....

    d Phoebus is completely in love with the young gypsy girl. .....

    e When Phoebus tries to make love to Esmeralda, she attacks him with a knife. .....

After you read

17 Imagine you are Esmeralda. Tell a friend about your visit to the house of the Gondelauriers. Why did they invite you in? Who was there? What happened?

18 Work with another student. Have this conversation.

Student A: You are Officer Phoebus. It is half past six and you are going to meet Esmeralda. But you have no money to pay for a hotel room. You meet a strange man in black in the street.

Student B: You are Father Frollo. You know Phoebus is going to meet Esmeralda at seven o'clock. You are afraid that she loves him. You want to hide in his room. Offer him money.

Chapter 4 (pages 28–35)

Before you read

19 Discuss these questions.

    a Is Phoebus dead, or is he going to die?

    b What will happen to Esmeralda now?

    c Why did Frollo attack Phoebus? Is he crazy?

While you read

20 Number these sentences, 1–6.

    a They take Esmeralda to the torture room.   .....

    b Madame Falourdel tells the judge what happened on March 29.   .....

    c Frollo tells Esmeralda that he loves her.   .....

    d Esmeralda says that she killed Phoebus.   .....

    e Frollo offers to save Esmeralda from death.   .....

    f Esmeralda says that she did not kill Phoebus.   .....

21 Why:

    a does Esmeralda say that she killed Phoebus?

    b does everyone believe that Esmeralda is a murderer?

    c does Frollo offer to save Esmeralda from death by hanging?

    d does Esmeralda refuse his help?

22 Imagine that you are Madame Falourdel. Tell the judge what happened on the night of March 29. Give your opinion of the prisoner.

Chapter 4 (pages 36–41)

Before you read

23 Esmeralda will die the following day. Frollo can save her life, but she refuses his help. Does she want to live? Can anyone save her now? What do you think?

24 Check the meaning of the word *sanctuary* in the Word List at the back of the book. Where in the story is a place of sanctuary for criminals?

While you read

25 Which is the right word?

    a Esmeralda sees that Phoebus is *dead / alive*.

    b Phoebus doesn't *hate / love* Esmeralda or Fleur-de-Lys—only himself.

    c Esmeralda is taken into the cathedral by *Frollo / Quasimodo*.

    d The crowd in the square are very *angry / happy* that Esmeralda is safe in the cathedral.

    e On his return to the cathedral, Frollo thinks that Esmeralda is *dead / with* Phoebus.

    f Quasimodo gives Esmeralda a *kiss / whistle*.

    g Frollo's love for Esmeralda is making him *mad / happy*.

26 Is Frollo really an evil person? Maybe he is only unhappy? What do you think?

27 How do these people feel? Give reasons for your answers.

    a Quasimodo, about Esmeralda

    b Esmeralda, about Quasimodo

    c Quasimodo, about Frollo

    d Frollo, about Quasimodo

28 Discuss why the whistle is important to the story.

Chapter 5

Before you read

29 Esmeralda is safe if she stays inside the cathedral. Discuss these questions.

    a How long can she stay there?

    b What will Frollo do?

    c Can Quasimodo protect her? Why (not)?

30 The chapter is called "Together in Death". Who will be together in death? Will the story have a happy ending or an unhappy one? How would you like the story to end? Tell the class.

While you read

31 Who:

    a does Gringoire ask to save Esmeralda? ....

    b will stop Father Claude from attacking Esmeralda? ....

    c throws stones at the crowd? ....

    d stops the fight? ....

    e comes to Esmeralda's room with Gringoire? ....

    f does Gringoire leave the boat with? ....

    g is Esmeralda's mother? ....

    h kills Sachette and Esmeralda? ....

After you read

32 Who says these words and why are they important in the story?

    a "This little shoe is the only thing that the gypsies left me."

    b "All that I ever loved!"

33 Work with another student. Have this conversation.

    Student A: You saw the attacks on the Cathedral, but you did not see Esmeralda's death. Speak to your friend about what you saw. Ask questions about Esmeralda.

    Student B: You did not see the attacks on the Cathedral. Ask your friend about them. Answer your friend's questions about the deaths of Esmeralda and Sachette.

34 Discuss these questions.

    a Is the end of the story a good one? Why (not)?

    b Would you like a different ending? What is it?

Writing

35 You are a reporter for a Paris newspaper. You were in the Great Hall today, January 6, 1482. Write a news report about what happened there.

36 You are Frollo. You have taken the young Quasimodo into the cathedral and you are teaching him. The head of the cathedral asks you for a report. He wants to know why you took this ugly hunchback boy into the cathedral. Give your reasons. Tell him what the boy has learned.

37 You are Fleur-de-Lys de Gondelaurier. Every day, you write in a notebook what you did that day. Write about the day Phoebus visited you and your friends. Write about the gypsy girl who danced.

38 You are Madame Falourdel, the hotel keeper. When Phoebus and Esmeralda are found in a room in your hotel, the police ask you for a full report of that evening. You must write about everything that happened. Who did you see? When? What did you hear? When? What did you think?

39 Who do you think is the most interesting person in this story? Write about that person. What are they like? What did they do? What happened to them? Why?

40 Imagine that you are looking for a husband. Choose one of these people: Phoebus, Gringoire, Frollo, Quasimodo. Write about the man. Give your reasons for choosing him.

41 A movie company wants to make a movie of this story, but the ending is too sad. Write a new, happier ending. Start from Sachette's realization that Esmeralda is her lost daughter.

42 Did you enjoy this book? Write about it for other students. Tell them about the book and why they should (not) read it.

WORD LIST

bell (n) a metal, cup-shaped thing. It makes a ringing sound when it is hit

cathedral (n) a very large church, the main church in a city

devil (n) a very bad person; an enemy of good

evil (adj) very bad and dangerous

flog (v) to hit someone with, for example, a piece of rope as a punishment

fool (n) a stupid person

goat (n) an ordinary farm animal that is kept for its wool, milk, and meat

gypsy (n) one of a group of people who follow an unusual, colorful way of life and usually travel around a lot

hang (v) to kill someone by dropping them with a rope around their neck

hump (n) a thick, rounded part on the back of a person or animal

hunchback (n) an impolite word for a person with a hump on their back

priest (n) a person who has studied the Christian religion and works for a Christian church

rope (n) very strong, thick, long material, used for tying things

sanctuary (n) a safe place for people in danger

skeleton (n) the hard inside part of a body which gives it a shape

sorcerer (n) an evil person who uses mysterious sciences

torture (v) to hurt a person many times as punishment or because you want information from them

tower (n) a tall, narrow building

whistle (n) something that makes a loud noise when air from your mouth moves through it

witch (n) a woman who can do very bad and mysterious things

Matilda
Roald Dahl

Matilda is a very clever little girl, but her terrible parents don't like her, and her head teacher, Miss Trunchbull, is very frightening. She isn't very happy. Then one day Matilda starts moving things with her eyes, and after that she isn't afraid of anybody! *Also a film starring Danny De Vito.*

Gladiator

Maximus is a general in the Roman army. After his last battle he wants to return to his family. But the new Emperor Commodus hates Maximus, and kills his family. Soon Maximus is a prisoner, then a slave, and finally a gladiator. When Emperor Commodus joins Maximus in the arena they fight for their lives. *This Oscar-winning film stars Russell Crowe.*

The Time Machine
H.G. Wells

The Time Traveller has built a time machine and has gone into the future to the year 802,701. He expects to find a better world with highly intelligent people and great inventions. Instead, he finds that people have become weak, child-like creatures. They dance and sing and wear flowers. They seem happy, but why are they so frightened of the dark? And who or what has taken his time machine? Will the Time Traveller ever be able to return to the present?

There are hundreds of Penguin Readers to choose from – world classics, film adaptations, modern-day crime and adventure, short stories, biographies, American classics, non-fiction, plays ...

For a complete list of all Penguin Readers titles, please contact your local Pearson Longman office or visit our website.

www.penguinreaders.com

Longman Dictionaries

Express yourself with confidence!

Longman has led the way in ELT dictionaries since 1935. We constantly talk to students and teachers around the world to find out what they need from a learner's dictionary.

Why choose a Longman dictionary?

Easy to understand

Longman invented the Defining Vocabulary – 2000 of the most common words which are used to write the definitions in our dictionaries. So Longman definitions are always clear and easy to understand.

Real, natural English

All Longman dictionaries contain natural examples taken from real-life that help explain the meaning of a word and show you how to use it in context.

Avoid common mistakes

Longman dictionaries are written specially for learners, and we make sure that you get all the help you need to avoid common mistakes. We analyse typical learners' mistakes and include notes on how to avoid them.

Innovative CD-ROMs

Longman are leaders in dictionary CD-ROM innovation. Did you know that a dictionary CD-ROM includes features to help improve your pronunciation, help you practice for exams and improve your writing skills?

For details of all Longman dictionaries, and to choose the one that's right for you, visit our website:

www.longman.com/dictionaries